Contents

Unit 1	The diagonal join to v and w	4
Unit 2	The diagonal join to p and y	6
Unit 3	The diagonal join to b and t	8
Unit 4	The diagonal join to d and g	10
Unit 5	The diagonal join to e	12
Unit 6	Joining words with diagonal joins	14
Unit 7	The horizontal join to v and w	16
Unit 8	The horizontal join to p and y	18
Unit 9	The horizontal join to b and t	20
Unit 10	The horizontal join to d and g	22
Unit 11	The horizontal join to e	24
Unit 12	Joining words	26
Unit 13	Starting with break letters	28
Unit 14	Break letters within words	30
Unit 15	Punctuation focus	32
WriteWell challenge 1		34
WriteWell challenge 2		35

The diagonal join to v and w

This join goes from letters that end on the baseline to letters that start at the short letter line.

The letters **v** and **w** have sloping lines. Take the join up to the short letter line. Then slope down to form the letter **v** or **w**.

av aw

Try it

Trace and then write the joined letters.

WriteWell

Book Seven
More Joining

Handwriting Stage 3 | Year 2

Schofield & Sims

Name

Welcome to this book

The **WriteWell** series will help you to develop good handwriting habits. As you work through the series, you will learn how to improve your handwriting and develop your own style.

This is **Book 7**. In this book, you will learn how to join more letters, building upon the joins you have already learnt and practised in **Book 6**.

More joins

As before, you will tackle the letters in groups according to the shape of join needed to link them together: diagonal joins and horizontal joins. You will also learn to join some trickier letters, such as those to the letter **e**.

Diagonal join to **e**
(for letters that end at the baseline)

Horizontal join to **e**
(for letters that end at the short letter line)

short letter line
baseline   ue   le   oe   ve

As in Book 6, a **red dot** is used to show the starting point of the first letter, and a **purple dot** is used to show the starting point of the second letter. A **purple line** is used to show the join.

You will also learn about break letters. These are letters that are not joined in the normal way because of their shape, or because they finish on the left-hand side.

Break letter at the beginning of a word

Break letter in the middle of a word

bad

night

Checking your work

When you finish a unit, look back at your work. Do your joins look like the example? Circle your best join and then choose one to improve.

Before you start

Check that your body is in the correct position for writing. Ask an adult to help you.

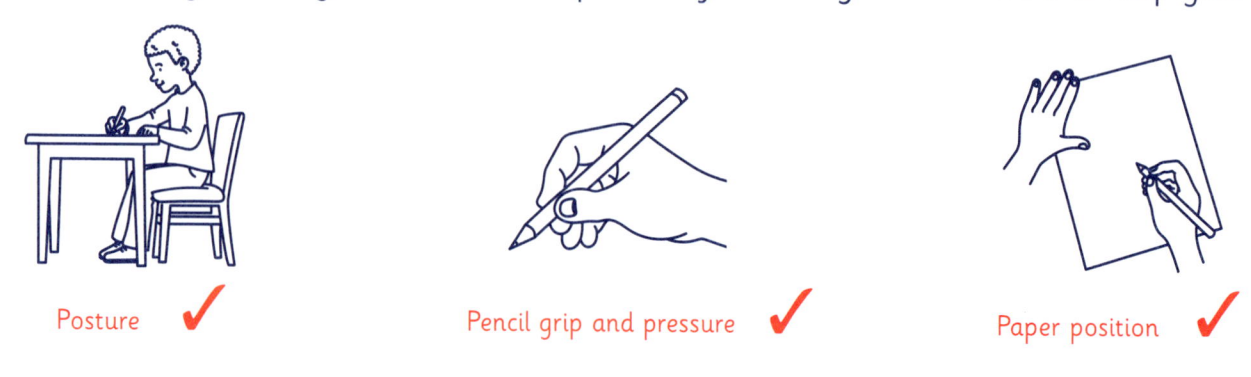

Posture ✓   Pencil grip and pressure ✓   Paper position ✓

Practise it

Trace and then write the joined words.

few few few five five five

paw paw paw save save save

live live give new live

evil evil evil twin twin

Apply it

Write the word *have* to complete each fact about lions. Then copy the facts.

Lions _have_ four paws.

paws.

Lions _don't_ long claws.

claws.

Lions _donot_ to eat a lot.

to

Lions _____ to chew raw meat.

Lions

The diagonal join to p and y

The letters **p** and **y** have tails that hang below the baseline.

Take the join up to the short letter line. Then come down to form the letter **p** or **y** so that the body sits on the line and the tail hangs below.

ap ay

Try it

Trace and then write the joined letters.

ap ap

ay ay

ip ip

up up

ly ly

ey ey

Practise it

Trace and then write the joined words.

cup	day

tip	clap

sly	only

key	chip

Apply it

Write a word to complete each exclamation. Then copy the exclamations.

money	honey	monkey	valley

What yummy _____!

What a funny _____!

What a lot of _____!

What a sunny _____!

Book 7 | More Joining

The diagonal join to b and t

To join to tall letters such as **b** and **t**, take the join up to the tall letter line. Then trace down to form the tall letter.

Remember the letter **t** is not as tall as the other tall letters.

ab at

Try it

Trace and then write the joined letters.

ab ab

at at

ub ub

it it

nt nt

lt lt

Practise it

Trace and then write the joined words.

cub   knit

flat   dab

slab   tilt

belt   ant

Apply it

Write a word to complete each command. Then copy the commands.

> Plant   Rub   Let   Catch

_____ the bulbs in a tub.

_____ all the ice melt.

_____ out the faint chalk line.

_____ the train at ten.

Book 7 | More Joining

The diagonal join to d and g

The letters **d** and **g** start with a curve like the letters **a**, **c** and **o**.

Take the join up towards the short letter line and curve over to the start of the letter. Then come back and trace round to form the letter **d** or **g**.

id ig

Try it

Trace and then write the joined letters.

id id

ig ig

nd nd

ld ld

ug ug

ng ng

Practise it

Trace and then write the joined words.

dig find

lid thing

tug plug

old mild

Apply it

Write the word **and** to complete each sentence. Then copy the sentences.

It was a wild _and_ windy day.

A bell rang both day ___ night.

The king was kind ___ rich.

One sad child ran ___ hid.

Book 7 I More Joining

The diagonal join to e

The letter **e** starts nearer the baseline than the other round letters. When joining to **e**, slope the join up at an angle to reach the start of the **e**. Then curve round to make the loop.

Remember the letter **e** is the same size as the other short letters.

ie   ue   le

Try it

Trace and then write the joined letters.

ie   ie

ue   ue

le   le

he   he

me   me

ce   ce

Practise it

Trace and then write the joined words.

due   met

her   tile

ice   lied

leg   help

Apply it

Write a word to complete each noun phrase. Then copy the phrases.

space   fence   slice   race

a _____ of cake

a motor car _____

a rocket in _____

a _____ with a gate

Book 7 | More Joining

Joining words with diagonal joins

Some words have endings such as **–ed** or **–er** added to them.

First join the letters in the main word. Then, without lifting your pencil, join to the ending. Try to join all the letters smoothly.

add ed → *added*

Try it

1 Trace and then continue the joined pattern.

eded

2 Trace and then write the joined words.

add → *added*

end → *ended*

call → *called*

melt → *melted*

lick → *licked*

talk → *talked*

Practise it

Trace and then write the joined words.

ended   *hated*

liked   *melted*

called   *landed*

talked   *named*

Apply it

Write a verb to complete each sentence. Then copy the sentences.

> heated   baked   hiked   cleaned

A baker _____ many cakes.

The cleaner _____ my table top.

The hiker _____ up the tall hill.

The heater _____ the kennel.

Book 7 | More Joining

The horizontal join to v and w

Use horizontal joins to join letters that finish at the short letter line to the next letter. You have already learnt to join from **o** to **i** and **u**.

Take the join across from **o** to the start of the new letter. Go straight down to form the letter **i** or **u**. Slope down to form the letter **v** or **w**.

oi ou ov ow

Try it

1 Trace and then write the joined letters.

   oi oi

   ou ou

   ov ov

   ow ow

2 Trace and then continue the joined patterns.

   vvvv vvvv

   wow wow

Practise it

Trace and then write the joined words.

low　　　　　　　　　love

now　　　　　　　　　oval

own　　　　　　　　　over

owl　　　　　　　　　dove

Apply it

Write a word to complete each sentence. Then copy the story.

> down　town　now　slow

Once, a clown was on his way to _____ . He drove _____ a hill and over a river. He could not _____ down! What would he do _____ ?

The horizontal join to p and y

Take the horizontal join across to the start of the letters **p** and **y**. Then go down to form the letter.

Make sure the body sits on the baseline and the tail hangs below.

op oy

Try it

1 Trace and then write the joined letters.

op op

oy oy

vy vy

wy wy

2 Trace and then continue the joined patterns.

wpwp wpwp

oyop oyop

Practise it

Trace and then write the joined words.

toy   flop

joy   stop

ivy   boy

hop   loop

Apply it

Write an adjective to complete each sentence. Then copy the sentences.

chewy   snowy   wavy   navy

The meat is far too _____ .

It was a cold and _____ day.

Davy wore a _____ blue top.

The boy had _____ hair.

Book 7 | More Joining   19

The horizontal join to b and t

To join to tall letters such as **b** and **t**, take the join across and up to the tall letter line. Come back down to form the tall letter.

Remember the letter **t** is not as tall as the other tall letters.

ob   ot

Try it

1 Trace and then write the joined letters.

    ob ob

    ot ot

    oth oth

    wt wt

2 Trace and then continue the joined patterns.

    vbvb vbvb

    wbwb wbwb

Practise it

Trace and then write the joined words.

hot　　　　　　　　　　　slot

both　　　　　　　　　　　blob

job　　　　　　　　　　　note

rob　　　　　　　　　　　sob

Apply it

Write a word to complete each picture caption. Then copy the captions.

newt　　sloth　　otter　　robin

a spotted _____

a slow brown _____

an _____ in the wild

a _____ in winter

Book 7 | More Joining　　　　　　　21

The horizontal join to d and g

To join to round letters such as **d** and **g**, take the join across and over to the start of the round letter. Trace back and go round to form the letter.

The join should create a space so the letters do not touch.

od og

Try it

1 Trace and then write the joined letters.

od od

og og

ood ood

wd wd

2 Trace and then continue the joined patterns.

oodod oodod

oogog oogog

Practise it

Trace and then write the joined words.

log plod

nod clog

food dog

odd flog

Apply it

Write a word to complete each sentence. Then copy the story.

> stood   flood   wooden

The _____ water was deep. A crowd _____ to watch it. A _____ shed sailed down the road. How odd it looked!

Book 7 | More Joining

The horizontal join to e

The letter **e** starts nearer to the baseline than other short letters.

To join to the letter **e**, the horizontal join must slope down to reach the start of the letter. From there, curve up to form the loop.

oe   ve   we

Try it

1   Trace and then write the joined letters.

   oe   oe

   ve   ve

   we   we

   ove   ove

2   Trace and then continue the joined patterns.

   veve   veve

   oeoe   oeoe

Practise it

Trace and then write the joined words.

vet　　　　　　　　　　well

eve　　　　　　　　　　toe

wet　　　　　　　　　　live

ever　　　　　　　　　　five

Apply it

Write the word **lived** to complete each sentence. Then copy the sentences.

A troll _lived_ in a cave.

A spider _____ in a web.

A poet _____ in a tower.

An old lady _____ in a shoe.

Book 7 | More Joining　　　25

Joining words

Use all the joins you have learnt to join words. Look for groups of letters that you can join and then join the groups together. Try to flow smoothly through the word.

tow el → towel

Try it

Trace the groups of letters and the joined words. Then write the words again fully joined.

tow el → towel

new er → newer

eve nt → event

le vel → level

moth er → mother

wall ow → wallow

won der → wonder

Practise it

Trace and then write the joined words.

allow   voice

fewer   cover

never   annoy

other   wallet

Apply it nation   ~~wallet~~

Write a word to complete each sentence. Then copy the story.

louder   wondered   voice

One day a man heard a voice coming from a cave. It was much louder than a lion. He hid and _____ what it could be.

Starting with break letters

These letters are break letters. They do not join to the next letter.

If a word starts with a break letter, write it and then lift your pencil and move it to the start of the next letter. Do not leave a space.

b g p j y q s x z

Try it

Trace and then write the words starting with break letters.

bad bad

got got

peg peg

jab jab

yet yet

sob sob

zap zap

Practise it

Trace and then write the joined words.

pig			yelp

bit			jolt

get			zip

quit			sell

Apply it

Write the words to complete each list sentence. Then copy the sentences.

> golden   silver   yellow   pink

I paint a blue summer sky, a _____ sun and a _____ sandy beach.

I paint a black sky, a _____ moon and a snug _____ quilt.

Book 7 | More Joining   29

Break letters within words

If a word has a break letter in it, join to the break letter but do not join it to the next letter. Lift your pencil and move to the next letter.

The letters **x** and **z** are special, as there is no join to or from them.

night amaze

Try it

Trace and then write the words with break letters.

night night

amaze amaze

table table

simple simple

crayon crayon

squeal squeal

vixen vixen

Practise it

Trace and then write the joined words with break letters.

player   *cycle*

empty   *cable*

squeak   *magic*

excite   *lazy*

Apply it

Write a word to complete each phrase. Then copy the phrases.

> edge   fudge   sledge   badge

dogs pulling a _____

a huge box of _____

Sophie's age on a _____

an axe with a sharp _____

Punctuation focus

Commas are used in lists. They sit on the baseline like full stops.

Apostrophes are used in contractions in place of a missing letter. The apostrophe sits just under the tall letter line. The letters on either side of the apostrophe are not joined.

we have → *we've*

Try it

1 Trace and then continue the punctuation pattern.

2 Trace the joined words. Then write the contractions.

we have → *we've*

I will → *I'll*

do not → *don't*

let us → *let's*

he is → *he's*

is not → *isn't*

32

Practise it

Trace and then write the contractions.

I'll   *can't*

I'm   *didn't*

she's   *that's*

it's   *we're*

Apply it

Write a contraction from **Practise it** above to complete each sentence. Then copy the sentences on to the postcard.

Dear Joe, Beth, Rob and Sita,

_____ camping in Devon with Mum. Today _____ cold and wet. We _____ swim, fish or go to the beach.

~ Postcard ~

Book 7 | More Joining

WriteWell challenge 1

Copy the rhyme in your best handwriting. Draw pictures and patterns in the border to go with your rhyme.

The wind

The wind came out to play one day.

She swept the clouds out of her way.

She blew the leaves and off they flew.

The trees bent low and branches too.

She blew the sailing ships at sea.

She took my kite away from me.

WriteWell challenge 2

Imagine you are Goldilocks and write a letter to the Three Bears to say sorry. Use your best handwriting and join letters where you can.

Dear Mr and Mrs Bear,

I am writing to _____

_____

I am sorry that I _____

_____

I hope _____

_____

From _____

P.S. Tell Baby Bear _____

_____

_____

_____

Book 7 | More Joining

35

Book Seven
More Joining

WriteWell

- Stage 1 — Shape
- Stage 2 — Space, size and sitting on the line
- **Stage 3 — Stringing together and slant**
- Stage 4 — Speed and style

Schofield & Sims WriteWell is a complete course designed to guide children from their first steps in mark-making towards the development of secure, fluent and comfortable joined handwriting that can be adapted for a range of purposes.

Handwriting is a complex process that requires the simultaneous use of cognitive, physical and perceptual skills. As development can vary greatly from child to child, **Schofield & Sims WriteWell** splits learning into manageable modules, offering you the flexibility to select the appropriate book for your child's needs. Young writers can then move through the programme at their own pace as their handwriting skills flourish – a highly personalised approach that ensures a confident foundation for every child.

This is WriteWell 7: More Joining. In this book, children will learn how to join more letters, building upon the horizontal and diagonal joins they have already learnt in WriteWell 6. This book includes 15 teaching units, each containing activities that gradually increase in difficulty, and two summative WriteWell Challenge tasks, designed to showcase new learning and encourage children to take pride in their handwriting skills.

Published by Schofield & Sims Ltd,
7 Mariner Court, Wakefield, West Yorkshire WF4 3FL, UK

This edition copyright © Schofield & Sims Ltd, 2019. First published in 2019

Author: Carol Matchett. Carol Matchett has asserted her moral rights under the Copyright, Designs and Patents Act, 1988, to be identified as the author of this work.

British Library Cataloguing in Publication Data
A catalogue record for this book is available from the British Library.

All rights reserved. No part of this publication may be reproduced, stored in a retrieval system, or transmitted in any form or by any means, electronic, mechanical, photocopying, recording or otherwise, without either the prior permission of the publisher or a licence permitting restricted copying in the United Kingdom issued by the Copyright Licensing Agency Limited, 5th Floor, Shackleton House, Hay's Galleria, 4 Battle Bridge Lane, London SE1 2HX.

Design by Oxford Designers & Illustrators Ltd. Cover design by Ledgard Jepson Ltd
Printed in the UK by Page Bros (Norwich) Ltd

Schofield & Sims

For further information and to place your order visit www.schofieldandsims.co.uk
or telephone 01484 607080

ISBN 978 07217 1639 8
£3.95 (Retail price)

ISBN 978-07217-1639-8